MARGARET PETERSON HADDIX

ALL ABOUT THE AUTHOR™

MARGARET PETERSON HADDIX

MARY-LANE KAMBERG

ROSEN
PUBLISHING®

New York

For my first writing mentors, Lois Daniel and Deborah Shouse

Published in 2014 by The Rosen Publishing Group, Inc.
29 East 21st Street, New York, NY 10010

Copyright © 2014 by The Rosen Publishing Group, Inc.

First Edition

Library of Congress Cataloging-in-Publication Data

Kamberg, Mary-Lane, 1948–
Margaret Peterson Haddix/Mary-Lane Kamberg. — First edition.
    pages cm. — (All About the Author)
Includes bibliographical references and index.
ISBN 978-1-4777-1765-3 (library binding)
1. Haddix, Margaret Peterson—Juvenile literature. 2. Women authors, American—Biography—Juvenile literature. 3. Young adult fiction—Authorship—Juvenile literature. I. Title.
PS3558.A31187Z73 2014
813'.54—dc23
[B]
                                                                    2013014576

Manufactured in the United States of America

CPSIA Compliance Information: Batch #W14YA: For further information, contact Rosen Publishing, New York, New York, at 1-800-237-9932.

CONTENTS

As a child, Margaret Peterson Haddix was an avid reader. Not too long after she learned to read, she started writing her own stories. From a fledgling writer in second or third grade, she has become a popular, award-winning author of books for children and young adult readers.

In more than thirty books, the author takes on a variety of topics. On one end of the scale, she has written about a silly family situation with light, funny dialogue. On the other, she has written about violent times in the past, as well as dark, future worlds. Her subject matter has included child abuse, workplace issues, and religious cults. And her time periods run from historic, to current time, to the future.

Book reviewers and award judges like her work, too. Reviewers have praised her talent for creating believable characters. They also applaud her suspenseful, page-turning plots with plenty of twists and turns. Her books have won awards from such organizations as the American Booksellers, American Library Association, International Reading Association, and Young Adult Library Services Association.

As a child, Margaret read books of all genres, including some handed down from her parents and grandparents. She also read her local newspaper and *Time* magazine.

Margaret Peterson Haddix began writing as a child, soon after she learned to read. Today, she is one of the most popular authors for middle-grade and middle-school readers.

Margaret started writing in elementary school. She wrote stories and poetry that she hid from friends and family. Her dream was to become a professional writer. However, she did not think that writing books for a living was a choice open to her. She was a farm girl. No one she knew worked as a writer. All the authors she knew about lived in big cities like New York and Los Angeles. Still, that's what she wanted to do.

In college, Margaret majored in English, focusing on creative writing and journalism. Journalism seemed to be a career choice where she could use her talent as a writer. She began her career in journalism, working as an intern at several newspapers during her college years. Her first two jobs after graduation were as a newspaper copy editor and general assignment reporter, but her true love was writing fiction. At first she wrote short stories for adult readers.

Her first ideas for novels, however, involved teenage characters, so she unintentionally fell into writing for young readers. Once she realized her dream of publishing a novel, she left the world of newspaper reporting behind. Since then, she has stuck to writing fiction.

Today, Haddix is a full-time professional writer. She is counted among the most popular authors for young readers of elementary and middle school age. And many of her books appeal to readers of all ages.

Overall, Haddix's approach to writing is simple. "I love books," she says on her Web site. "I love making up stories and playing around with words and imagining interesting people in interesting situations."

CHAPTER ONE

REAL LIFE

Do you like to read science fiction? Historical? Contemporary? Or do you not like to read at all? Are you in elementary, middle, or high school?

Margaret Peterson Haddix has a book for you.

The *New York Times* best-selling author is best known for two series: *The Missing* and *The Shadow Children*. *The Missing* is a time-travel sequence. *The Shadow Children* are books about children who live in hiding because the oppressive government prohibits families from having more than two children.

The rest of Haddix's thirty-plus novels cross genres. Some appeal to elementary school readers, others to middle school and high school readers. Most of her books are classified as young adult (YA) fiction. They are generally marketed to readers between the ages of twelve and eighteen. However, some YA novels are marketed to readers as young as ten years and as old as twenty-five.

MARGARET PETERSON
HADDIX

New York Times Bestselling Author

THE MISSING
FOUND

Rewriting the past to save the future

The Missing is a time travel series about children lost in time. Haddix got the idea for the novel when she landed after an airline trip and couldn't remember what city she was in.

Haddix's books for middle-grade readers include *The Girl with 500 Middle Names, Say What?, Because of Anya*, and *Dexter the Tough*. In addition to her series novels, Haddix has such other young adult titles as *Leaving Fishers, Uprising, The Always War*, and *Full Ride*.

GROWING UP

The award-winning author grew up in a family of storytellers and bookworms. So, even though her family members hate to write themselves, there is little surprise that she loved books and became a writer.

Margaret was born on April 9, 1964. Her mother, Merilee Grace Greshel Peterson, was a nurse. Her father, John Albert Peterson, was a farmer. He often told stories to his four children. Margaret has an older brother, as well as a younger brother and younger sister.

One tale her father told involved a family member who got kidnapped. Another was about a boy

The Rinard Covered Bridge is close to where Margaret Peterson Haddix grew up in southwestern Ohio. The area is known for its agriculture and picturesque views.

who took possum meat to the school cafeteria. Still another was about his childhood friends who survived lying on a railroad bridge while a train rumbled over them.

"I always thought that becoming a storyteller would be the grandest thing in the world," Haddix said in an interview with *Something About the Author*. "But I didn't want just to tell stories, I wanted to write them down."

The family farm lay between the towns of Washington Court House and Sabina in southwestern Ohio. The population of Washington Court House was 14,192 in the 2010 Census, according to the U.S. Census Bureau. In the same census, the town of Sabina's population was only 2,564. The Petersons raised corn, soybeans, wheat, hogs, chickens, and cattle. As children, Margaret and her brothers and sister took for granted that they had their own pony.

They often played with the farm animals. Margaret's mother loves to tell the story of the time when Margaret was all dressed and ready to go to church, but her mother couldn't find her. Margaret was out in the chicken coop playing with some baby chickens. She had to change clothes because she smelled like the chicken coop.

Margaret was happy to grow up on a farm. She had a lot of freedom and spent a lot of time outdoors. However, living in the country meant being a bit isolated from friends her age. Her closest friends lived several miles away. Because farms were so far apart, parents would have to drive children to one another's homes. So Margaret's brothers and sister were her main playmates. They became a close family, and that is reflected in many of her books, where siblings work together to solve things.

EARLY READING AND WRITING

The family's relative isolation created a good environment for reading. Margaret and her siblings loved to read at early ages. And Margaret has fond memories of the Washington Court House Carnegie Public Library, where she spent a lot of time as a child. Her schoolteachers also encouraged her reading.

Margaret read books that had belonged to her parents and grandparents when they were children. Her older brother and grandfather both loved science fiction, and they lent her their books. Margaret particularly liked character-driven books, where reading felt like "hanging out with a beloved friend," she said in a *1000 Wrongs* interview.

Adventure stories—also borrowed from her brothers—were more favorites, especially adventure novels with girls as main characters. But fiction wasn't all Margaret read. Newspapers and magazines held practical information. Even the backs of cereal boxes seemed interesting if she couldn't find anything else to read.

All Peterson family members read in their spare time, especially in summer. "When we went on family vacations, my parents were always saying things like, 'Would you guys stop reading for a minute and look out the window? That's the Grand Canyon we're driving past!'" Haddix says on her Web site.

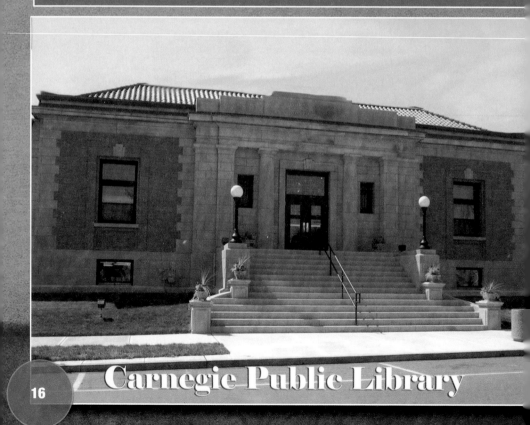

The Carnegie Public Library in Washington Court House, Ohio, was established with a 1901 grant from philanthropist Andrew Carnegie. The library grant was one of thousands issued between 1883 and 1929.

Carnegie Public Library

Her grandparents used to say the same thing to her mother when she was a child. And later, when Haddix had her own children, she said the same thing to them. She told *Reading Rockets* that she'd say, "Please put down *Harry Potter* for a moment! That's the Pacific Ocean out there!"

Reading was just Margaret's first step on the road to a writing career. It was a natural progression to go from loving books to wanting to create them herself. She started trying to write in second or third grade, making up stories and writing them down. She also wrote poetry in secret.

She wanted to be an author, but she didn't believe it was something "real" people got to do. All the adults she knew were farmers, nurses, teachers, dentists, housewives, or grocery clerks. However, she told Evi.com, "As soon as I realized that an actual person got to make up the books I loved so much, I decided that that was the job for me."

HIGH SCHOOL AND BEYOND

At Miami Trace High School in Washington Court House, Margaret got her first chance to publish her writing. She worked on the school newspaper.

The school was small, so she participated in many other activities as well. She acted in school plays and played flute and piccolo in the marching,

MARGARET PETERSON HADDIX'S FAVORITE BOOKS AT AGE TWELVE

As a child, Margaret Peterson Haddix read everything she could get her hands on. The variety of reading material included science fiction, realistic contemporary fiction, historical fiction, mysteries, and biographies. At age twelve, her favorite books included:

She, the Adventuress, by Dorothy Crayder
From the Mixed-Up Files of Mrs. Basil E. Frankweiler, by E. L. Konigsburg
A Little Princess, by Frances Hodgson Burnett
Anne of Green Gables, by L. M. Montgomery
Little Women, by Louisa May Alcott
The Long Journey, by Barbara Corcoran

Louisa May Alcott (*right*) was one of young Margaret's favorite authors. Alcott's most popular book is *Little Women,* now considered a classic for young readers.

pep, and symphonic bands. She sang in the school choir, ran track, and competed on a quick-recall team. Outside of school, she served on the county junior fair board and volunteered through her church and 4-H club. 4-H is a youth development organization that seeks to teach leadership, citizenship, and life skills with hands-on learning experiences.

During this time, she continued reading and writing. In addition to fiction, she read her local newspaper, *Time* magazine, and stories about the Great Depression. As with her choices in reading, she chose a variety of writing. She wrote both fiction and nonfiction. Throughout her education, teachers and college professors encouraged her writing. Some told her she should write for a living.

Still, she had to be practical about a career choice. The future author thought the only way she could make a living writing was to become a journalist. So when she enrolled at Miami University in Oxford, Ohio, she majored in English/creative writing and English/journalism. She also completed a bachelor's degree in history, which she told *Cynsations* was "just for fun."

During college she continued to write. And she continued to write both fiction and nonfiction. As a freshman she worked on her college newspaper.

WRITING CHALLENGES

Haddix faces challenges with every book—although they may be different with different books. Some include:

- Figuring out characters
- Working out the plot
- Deciding how to word passages
- Meeting deadlines
- Staying original in science fiction

And in 1983, she won honorable mention in *Seventeen* magazine's fiction writing contest.

She spent one semester studying in Luxembourg. On her Web site, she says, "Living in a foreign country is a great way to force yourself to really think about Who am I? What shaped me as a person? Why do I believe what I believe? What do I want out of life? What shaped all these people I see around me? Why do they believe what they believe? What do they want out of life?"

In summers between academic years, Margaret's professors helped arrange for internships at several newspapers. After her sophomore year, she worked at the *Urbana Daily Citizen* in Urbana, Ohio. After her junior year, she served an internship with the *Charlotte Observer* in Charlotte, North Carolina. And after her senior year, she worked for the *Indianapolis News* in Indianapolis, Indiana.

She graduated summa cum laude, which means "with highest honor," with university honors and English honors in 1987. Her first job was, a copy editor for the *Fort Wayne Journal Gazette* in Fort Wayne, Indiana. It seemed her future writing would fall under the heading of journalism.

THE WRITING LIFE

Wedding bells rang for Margaret Peterson and Doug Haddix in 1987. The couple met in college. Like his bride, the groom was interested in writing. He was a newspaper editor when they married. They moved to Indianapolis, Indiana, where Margaret Haddix took a job as a full-time reporter for the *Indianapolis News*.

She worked as a reporter until 1991. Most of that time, she was a general assignment reporter. That meant she covered a wide variety of stories on topics including fires, scientific breakthroughs, and politicians' news conferences—sometimes more than one topic in the same day.

In contrast, a beat reporter is someone who covers an assigned subject area. Examples of beats include local crime, a sports team, city government, religion, and health care.

"It was being a reporter that gave me the opportunity to meet lots of different people, in vastly different circumstances,"

Haddix says on her Web site. "It never failed to amaze me that I could sit down with people, and ask really, really nosy questions, and because I was from the newspaper, they would almost always answer."

SNEAKING IN SOME FICTION

But reporting didn't satisfy Haddix's desire to write fiction. On her Web site, she says, "Hearing so many different stories from so many different people—and witnessing so many different events—didn't just inspire me to write it all down. It also inspired me to play with different plots and characters and settings in my head. Facts weren't enough for me. I still also wanted fiction."

Haddix never changed facts for her newspaper stories. But after spending the whole day writing articles, she wrote different stories based on her imagination. "It wasn't always easy to write more in my time off work," she says on her Web site. "So during this time, I had a lot more ideas for fiction than I actually wrote down."

In 1991, Doug Haddix took a job as city editor of a newspaper in Danville, Illinois. The move complicated Margaret's career. If she wanted to work as a newspaper reporter, her husband would be her boss. Neither thought that would be a good idea. The two agreed that the situation offered a chance for Margaret to focus on fiction. They also decided

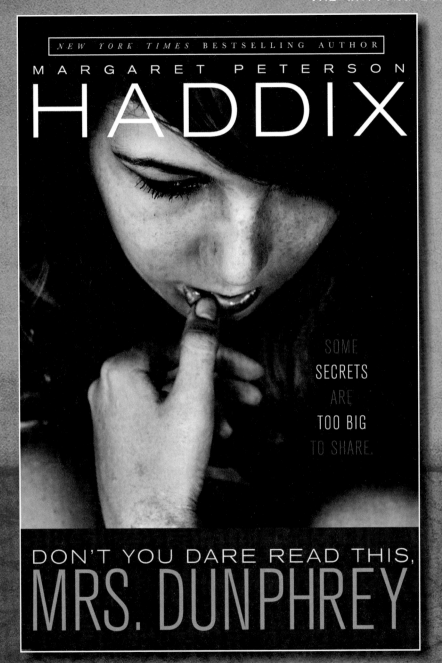

NEW YORK TIMES BESTSELLING AUTHOR

MARGARET PETERSON

HADDIX

SOME
SECRETS
ARE
TOO BIG
TO SHARE.

DON'T YOU DARE READ THIS,
MRS. DUNPHREY

Haddix based her second novel, *Don't You Dare Read This, Mrs. Dunphrey*, on a newspaper series she had written about abused and neglected children.

to start a family. To help with the family budget, she took freelance writing jobs for businesses and became a college instructor. She taught writing classes at the Danville Area Community College.

Haddix spent the rest of her time writing short fiction for adult readers. She hoped to be discovered as a short story writer. A short story is a piece of fiction, usually shorter than ten thousand words, focused on a single theme. She didn't get discovered, but she did win a trip to Hawaii for one of her stories.

In addition to that, she worked on the manuscripts for her first two books, *Running Out of Time* and *Don't You Dare Read This, Mrs. Dunphrey*. "Like most writers, I endured way more of the 'submit— then get rejected' cycle than I wanted to. (Because, who wants to endure any of it?)," she told Laurisa White Reyes of *1000 Wrongs*.

But success eluded Haddix for what she called "two years of depression and tears," in an interview with Kristy Eckert of *Capital Style*. Those two years made her wonder whether she was on the wrong path. "[Those years] didn't exactly feel like a stumble," she added. "They felt like I'd lost my footing completely and was sprawled flat on the ground being trampled by—I don't know what—vicious wolves, maybe?"

TIME TO WRITE

Finally, Haddix got a literary agent. A literary agent is an author's representative who looks for a publisher for a manuscript and negotiates the contract. A year after that, Simon & Schuster accepted her first two books for publication. The process from the first idea for *Running Out of Time* to publication took about four years. It took so long that when she sold her first two books, her daughter, Meredith, was eighteen months old, and Haddix was pregnant with her second child, Connor.

Taking care of the children presented a real challenge to her writing career. As reported in *Something About the Author*, she said, "I'm amused that I didn't think I had time to write before they were born."

For the first several years, she only wrote during naps, playdates, and preschool hours—times when she could have taken her own naps. So she developed strict criteria for everything she wrote: it had to be exciting enough to keep her awake. Today, her criteria remain the same. On her Web site, she says, "I know I have to write a story when the story keeps me awake at night, teases at the back of my brain all day, just won't let me go."

WORKING WITH EDITORS

Most modern authors work with different editors for different books. Unlike them, however, Margaret Peterson Haddix has worked with the same editor for all of her novels except *Into the Gauntlet*, which was published by Scholastic.

Her editor, David Gale, at Simon & Schuster picked up her first novel, *Running Out of Time*, and he has edited all of her other Simon & Schuster books. He even suggested that she write a book about the Triangle Shirtwaist Factory fire. The subsequent novel called *Uprising* was released in 2007.

In the past, writers often formed a long-term relationship with an editor. However, in today's publishing environment, those relationships are rare. Editors move on to other publishing houses, and sometimes writers do, too. That's why Haddix appreciates her association with Gale.

She said working together on so many books provides a level of comfort. "He can be pretty blunt with me when there is something he doesn't like," she said in the Reading *Rockets* interview. "He's not having to be very careful that he might offend me. Maybe that's good, maybe it's not. And then other times, I can trust him if I go to him with an idea. If he says yes or says no, I know that that's really how it is."

Firefighters raced on horse-drawn fire engines to answer the call to the Triangle Shirtwaist Factory, which caught fire on March 25, 1911. The tragedy is the subject of Haddix's novel *Uprising*.

WRITING FOR YOUNG AUDIENCES

The early novels Haddix wrote appealed to middle-grade and older readers. But Meredith and Connor were only in first and second grades. They begged her to write books for their age group. Her publisher also asked her to write chapter books for early readers. She wrote *The Girl with 500 Middle Names, Say What?, Dexter the Tough,* and *Because of Anya.* However, writing, editing, and publishing books takes a long time. When the books came out, Meredith and Connor were older and reading at a higher level.

In addition to urging their mother to write for a younger audience, Meredith and Connor helped in other ways. The author credits them and their friends with helping her with her early books. She volunteered in their elementary school and wrote about things she noticed in their classrooms.

Today, Haddix enjoys writing for a variety of readers in many genres. Sometimes she doesn't even think about who those readers are. If she's writing about an eight-year-old, for instance, she puts herself in the body of an eight-year-old. She uses an eight-year-old's vocabulary. She looks at things the way an eight-year-old would. The same pattern applies to characters of other ages for other audiences.

WRITING BOOKS IN A SERIES

Another challenge Haddix has encountered is writing books in a series. She plots each separately. But she struggles with knowing how much background to include in each book. She has written books for three series: Her own *The Missing* and *The Shadow Children*, and Scholastic's *39 Clues*. She told *Publisher's Weekly*, "I want book three to be a book you can pick up and enjoy even if you haven't read books one and two. And that's hard."

Writing series books was not her first plan. When she started writing novels, she saw each as a stand-alone book. However, when *Among the Hidden* came out in 1998, fans told her she should write a series about the characters. "It honestly took me a long time to see it that way," Haddix told *Reading Rockets*, "because to me the book was finished, I didn't have anything else to tell."

It took those fans, Haddix's husband, her brother, her agent, and her editor to convince her. She wrote more about Luke in *Among the Imposters*, the second book in the series, which came out in 2001. When she did, she learned that she felt comfortable with the protagonist and the new situation. Now, she likes to revisit characters. It gives her a chance to include ideas about them that didn't fit into earlier books in the series.

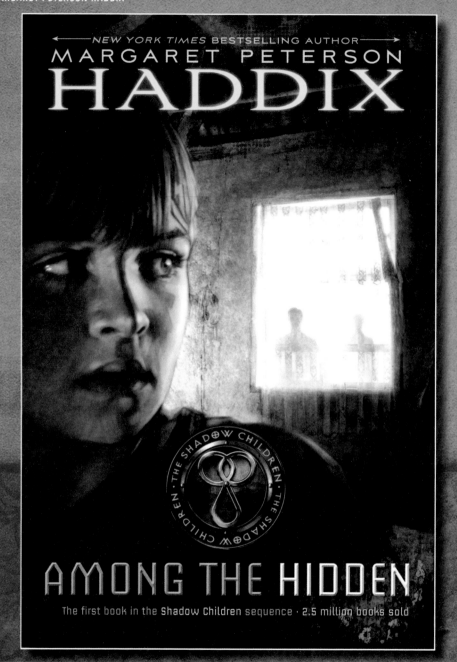

Writing series novels like *Among the Hidden* lets Haddix revisit characters and include details that didn't fit into earlier books. As of 2013, she had published seven novels in *The Shadow Children* series.

In fact, Haddix likes writing both types of novels. In some ways, writing a series is easier than writing a novel from scratch. Haddix likes being able to continue with the same characters. On the other hand, the author sometimes likes to write a stand-alone book and be able to say, "It's finished."

THREE

THE IMAGINARY LIFE

Have you ever become so involved in a book that the real world seems to slip away? Among readers and writers, this idea is called the fictive dream. It is a subconscious activity that is similar to daydreaming. The daydream, though, is guided by the author of a piece of fiction. The fictive dream happens when a reader becomes so absorbed in the world that the author created, the fiction seems to become reality. For this to happen, the reader and author enter into an unspoken contract called the willing suspension of disbelief.

CHAPTER

The willing suspension of disbelief means the reader knows the events in a novel never happened, but he or she makes the decision to believe them anyway—at least until the end of the book.

SUSPENDING DISBELIEF

The willing suspension of disbelief was first named by author Samuel Taylor Coleridge in 1817. It happens when a reader temporarily accepts fictional events and characters as "real," fully knowing that they are made up. The contract is necessary when a reader or audience member experiences a work of fiction or a drama.

According to Haddix, the first person who has to suspend disbelief and accept that whatever happens in this made-up world is true is the author. At times when she is writing, she thinks no one will believe what's happening. In the *Reading Rockets* interview, she said, "If I'm thinking that, of course they're not going to believe it because even I don't believe it...I can remember with my first book when I was sending it out and trying to get it published, some of the editors who rejected it were saying oh, this just isn't believable. And I'm like, but it happened, it really happened. And I'm like oh wait, no, it didn't."

WHERE IDEAS COME FROM

Early in Haddix's career when she was writing newspaper articles, she was also collecting ideas to write about. "My first three books all grew out of my work as a newspaper reporter," she told an interviewer from the Teen Book Festival. The author used the "what if technique" used by many authors to imagine a plot that was related to but different from real life.

One of the newspaper stories Haddix covered, for example, was about a living history museum called Connor Prairie. It is the site of a restored historical village near Indianapolis, Indiana. The people who worked there pretended to live in the 1800s all day. As part of her reporting, Haddix asked them what it was like to live in one century and work in the other. Some of them said that on slow days without many tourists, they almost forgot it *wasn't* the 1800s.

Haddix later told *Something About the Author*, "I kept wondering what it would be like if there was a historical village where all the tourists were hidden and the kids, at least, didn't know what year it really was."

She thought it was a good idea for a book. But it took several years to figure out the plot and write what became her first novel, *Running Out of Time*.

Haddix's second novel, *Don't You Dare Read This, Mrs. Dunphrey*, tells the story of Tish Bonner, a tough-talking student whose parents abandon her. Tish must write a journal for English class. Her teacher has promised not to read any parts marked, "Do Not Read." So, Tish marks that on every entry.

The idea for this book also grew out of the author's days as a reporter. Haddix had worked on a newspaper series where she interviewed more than twelve abused and neglected children. "Their stories haunted me for years," she told *Something About the Author*.

IDEAS FROM PERSONAL LIFE

Sometimes Haddix gets an idea for a book from events in her own life. For example, she got the idea for *Among the Hidden* when she and her husband were thinking about having a third child. She knew about China's one-child policy and thought about how that could affect families.

少生优生 幸福一生

中共双旺镇委员会
双旺镇人民政府

This sign refers to the Chinese government's limit of one child per family. The idea for *Among the Hidden* came from that fact and Haddix's real-life discussion with her husband about having a third child.

The novel is set in a totalitarian society that limits families to two children. Some families hide their subsequent offspring. The book was the first in *the Shadow Children* series, which had sold more than 2.5 million copies as of 2009, according to *Capital Style*. Luke, the twelve-year-old protagonist, has spent his entire life in hiding. His life changes when he meets another "third child" in hiding and decides to defy authority and seek a life where he has free will.

The idea for *Dexter the Tough* grew out of something the author read that a real student had written about a fight. The student wrote, "I am the new kid, I am tough, I have already beaten up a kid." The novel deals with the impression that would make on a new teacher—and how the teacher would deal with it.

The idea for *Found*, the first book in the time travel series *The Missing*, came from another real-life experience. Haddix had flown across six time zones one day. She woke up on the plane. At first she couldn't remember her destination or where she had come from. She thought that feeling would be a good idea to use in a book.

What if, she wondered, a mysterious kid felt the same way on an airplane? What if there were more than one kid? What if they were babies? What if the adults didn't know who they were either?

HADDIX AND PUBLISHER THREATEN LAWSUIT

Soon after Disney released the M. Night Shyamalan film *The Village* in 2004, fans and friends contacted Margaret Peterson Haddix. They had noticed parallels between the movie and her book *Running Out of Time*, which was published in 1995.

Both works are set in a nineteenth-century forest village. Both protagonists are young girls characterized as tomboys. Both plots involve the same secret that the adults keep from the children. And both plots have the same surprise ending.

Publisher Simon & Schuster and Haddix both told *USA Today* that they were weighing their options. One possibility was a lawsuit against the filmmakers for plagiarism because of the similarities. Plagiarism is claiming someone else's words or ideas as one's own without giving credit to the original source.

Spokespersons for both Disney and Shyamalan's production company, Blinding Edge Pictures, told Reuters the claim was "meritless." Shyamalan told IMDb.com, "The inspiration for the story comes from *Wuthering Heights* for period drama and *King Kong* for the community living in fear of predatory creatures."

A search found no record of a lawsuit being filed. However, another similarity between the works is the success of both projects. The novel sold over five hundred thousand copies in hardcover and paper-back, according to *Business News*. As of November 2004, the film with a reported $60 million budget had grossed more than $114 million, according to IMDb.com.

In *Found*, an airplane appears out of nowhere. All thirty-six passengers are babies. Airline personnel take the babies off the plane, and the plane instantly vanishes. The babies are adopted out. Thirteen years later, some adopted children discover that some-one—and some time—wants them back.

"I first became intrigued by the notion of a mys-terious planeload of babies," Haddix told Laurisa White Reyes from *1000 Wrongs*. "Then, once I figured out who those babies should be, I was fas-cinated by the idea of writing about kids who were raised in the twenty-first century getting to explore dangerous time periods of the past."

The time travel feature challenged Haddix. She had to make the series make sense. She had to fig-ure out how the future of the story would change if she changed the past. Would that change how the characters lived their lives?

HISTORY OFFERS IDEAS

For *Sabotaged*, Haddix's third book in *the Missing* series, she wanted to send characters Jonah, Katherine, and Andrea to Virginia Dare's Roanoke Colony. In studying the history of the settlement, she read about a theory that the lost colony was sabotaged from the beginning.

"I saw a great opportunity to draw parallels between the dangers and uncertainties and fears the original colonists faced, and the ones my own characters were facing," Haddix said at the 2010 National Book Festival.

The idea for another historical novel came from David Gale, Haddix's editor at Simon & Schuster. He suggested she write about the Triangle Shirtwaist Factory fire in New York City. The fire broke at 4:45 PM on March 25, 1911. Only 18 minutes later, 146 garment workers had died—mostly young women between the ages of 14 and 23, according to the AFL-CIO. Factory doors in the ten-story building had been locked to prevent theft. Many victims jumped from the eight, ninth, and tenth floors to their deaths on the concrete below.

The next morning, more than fifteen thousand garment workers walked off their jobs. They were

A stone marker commemorates the site of the historic Roanoke Colony, the first English settlement in the present-day United States. The site is the setting for *Sabotaged*, Haddix's third book in *The Missing* series.

joined by five thousand more the day after that. The total represented workers from five hundred factories, all according to the AFL-CIO. Later, the New York legislature enacted workplace safety laws, and several other states followed its lead.

Haddix's stand-alone book *Uprising* was published in 2007.

THE RESEARCHER'S LIFE

"Digging for details." That's what Haddix calls her research for a novel. She reads books, phones experts, and checks online sources. For some books, the author travels to the location where her fictional events take place.

The importance of research in Haddix's novels depends on the book. Some books require very little. Others need a lot.

RESEARCHING THE PAST

Running Out of Time is one novel that needed extensive investigation. Haddix enjoyed studying history in college, so the task is familiar and fun for her. "Unfortunately for my purposes, most history books tell about presidents and wars,"

History has no record of seven years in Elizabethan playwright William Shakespeare's life. The gap gave Haddix a chance to let her characters interact with "the Bard" in *Into the Gauntlet.*

she said in *Something About the Author*. "Not what kinds of utensils ordinary people would use, or what clothes a girl on the frontier might wear." She read a lot about the early 1800s, just to find references like those.

For *Into the Gauntlet*, the tenth book in the *39 Clues* series from Scholastic, Haddix researched William Shakespeare's life. She looked for details young readers would relate to, as well as ideas for the plot. During the search, Haddix learned about what is called the Elizabethan poet and playwright's "lost years." It's a seven-year period in Shakespeare's life where no records exist. She used that time frame to let her characters interact with the sixteenth-century writer.

Sometimes when Haddix starts to study a historical era, she thinks she's not particularly interested in that time period—or even that it's boring. However, as soon as she starts to research, she often finds the time period interesting after all.

That's what happened when she was researching *Sent*, the second book in *the Missing* series, which is set in the Middle Ages. "I always thought of the Middle Ages as dull," she told *Reading Rockets*. "They were not. There were so many exciting things going on and so many power struggles and really dramatic events that affected people's lives."

IS TIME TRAVEL POSSIBLE?

Renowned physicist, cosmologist, and author Stephen Hawking explained the principle of time travel at the Seattle Science Festival on June 16, 2008:

"We are all travelling forward in time anyway. We can fast-forward by going off in a rocket at high speed and return to find everyone on Earth much older or dead. Einstein's general theory of relativity seems to offer the possibility that we could warp space-time so much that we could travel back in time. However, it is likely that warping would trigger a bolt of radiation that would destroy the spaceship and maybe the space-time itself. I have experimental evidence that time travel is not possible. I gave a party for time-travelers, but I didn't send out the invitations until after the party. I sat there a long time, but no one came."

The author used the power struggles to compare the battle for the English crown to problems some middle school students have when they want to be popular.

PRIMARY SOURCES

Primary sources are original materials such as artifacts or information obtained from live, written, or recorded origins. Primary sources offer new thoughts, new information, or new discoveries. They come from the time period that is contemporary with the topic being studied. That may be a historic era or modern times.

Examples include:

- Interviews
- Diaries
- Birth certificates, wills, marriage licenses
- Letters, e-mail, list serves
- Speeches
- Newspaper articles
- Professional journal articles
- Artifacts (fossils, furniture, tools, clothing)
- Trial transcripts
- Photographs
- Audio/video recordings
- Patents

Students search microfilm reels to learn about primary source documents for their history class in Haddix's home state of Ohio. Haddix uses primary sources to research subjects in her historical novels.

CREATING HISTORIC PERSPECTIVE

Haddix likes to include facts from the past in some of her fiction to make history come alive for her readers. Some students think history is boring. But in a novel, readers can put themselves in the place of a character in a particular period. The impact is greater than one from reading a history textbook. The readers gain a historical view.

Haddix has noticed that many issues of the past are still issues today. For example, the main topic in *Uprising* is dealing with poor immigrants coming to the United States in the early 1900s and taking jobs. As Haddix researched the time period, she noticed that the same immigration debate was occurring today.

"A hundred years, and it's the same issue," she told *Reading Rockets*. "We still haven't figured out how to deal with this and how to be fair to every-body. But on the bright side, the other issue was women's rights. Women were trying to get the right to vote at that point. So I reminded myself that we have made progress in the last hundred years. Women can vote now."

Not all research is historic. *The Missing* series, which is about time travel, required both historical and scientific research. The characters go back into

Immigrants to the United States crowded the decks of ships like the S.S. *Amerika* in the early 1900s. The immigrants landed on Ellis Island and entered the country to look for work.

various periods in history. Haddix studied everything she could about each era so that the details would be accurate. She also looked into scientific theories about how time travel would be possible and addressed some of those theories in her books.

ASK THE EXPERTS

Haddix's newspaper reporting experience helps her research her novels. She often phones experts to ask questions. That saves time compared with searching through a stack of library books. However, her calls can sometimes sound embarrassing.

When writing *Don't You Dare Read This, Mrs. Dunphrey*, the author wanted information about how authorities would deal with a child whose parents abandoned her. She called a social worker at a child welfare agency. During the conversation, she kept repeating that she was working on fiction and wasn't planning to desert her children. She got the answers she was looking for, but she was never sure whether the social worker thought she was a bit crazy.

To make the plot believable in *Dexter the Tough*, Haddix interviewed real-life teachers. She wanted to know how they would deal with a new student who introduced himself as a tough kid who had already beaten up someone. She interviewed several teachers, including her own child's fifth-grade teacher. The

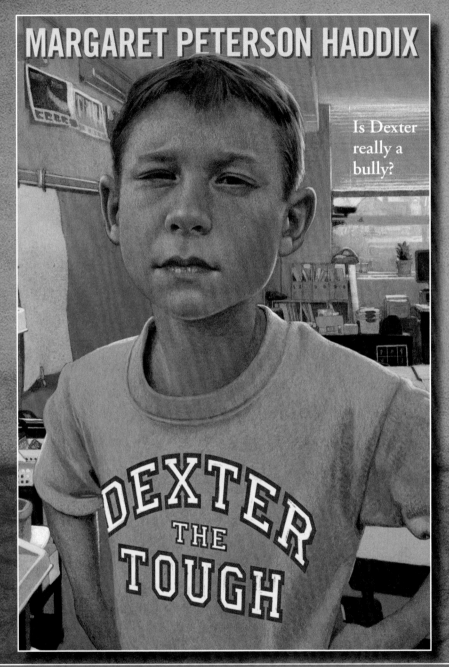

MARGARET PETERSON HADDIX

Is Dexter really a bully?

DEXTER THE TOUGH

To research the novel *Dexter the Tough*, Haddix interviewed several teachers, including her own child's teacher, to see how they would handle a new student like Dexter.

information helped her create the imaginary teacher's believable reaction.

In the novel, the teacher gives Dexter a long-term writing assignment. The process helps her understand him and helps him come to terms with the issues in his life. In a *Booklist* review of the novel, Kay Weisman said, "Through Dexter's writing assignment, readers come to understand much about authorship, revision, and point of view."

RELIABLE SOURCES

Haddix is both appreciative and wary of the World Wide Web as a source of information. The Internet was useful when the author was working at home on *Uprising*, which is set in the 1900s. She found original newspaper articles from the period in far less time than it would have taken at a physical library.

However, she realizes that much of the easy-to-access information on the Internet is incorrect. So, she starts her research on the Internet to give her a sense of the topic and then follows up with books or primary sources. Primary sources are such original materials as interviews, original documents, and artifacts that are free from another's evaluation— sources that other research is based on.

After satisfying herself that her information is accurate, Haddix sometimes does quick fact checks online. But she's always cautious about her sources of information.

REAL-TIME TRAVEL

Haddix also uses original research for her books. She has gone on location—traveling to her novels' settings. For *Running Out of Time*, she returned to Connor Prairie, the historic site she had visited as a reporter. "I acted like a spy," she said at the 2010 National Book Festival, "though I didn't want to copy too much from there because I really like Conner Prairie. I didn't want anyone thinking that I thought it was an evil place!"

The author also traveled to the settings for *Sabotaged* and *Into the Gauntlet*, both released in 2010. "For *Sabotaged* I went to Roanoke Island in North Carolina during the course of my research," she said at the National Book Festival. "I really tried to imagine what it would have been like on that spot more than four hundred years ago—both for the English settlers and for the natives."

Haddix took her family along to London and Stratford-upon-Avon for *Into the Gauntlet*. She saw all the places her characters visited. And she got help from her children, who helped her find places where someone might hide a clue.

Original research includes experimentation. Haddix has done that, too. "Sometimes I get a little

Haddix and her family visited Stratford-upon-Avon in Warwickshire, England, to research *Into the Gauntlet*. Her children explored the market town, looking for good places for characters to hide clues.

carried away trying to research my books," she told the Teen Book Festival. "One time I zipped myself into a suitcase to see if it would be possible for a character to do this in my book *Escape from Memory*. This wouldn't have been so bad, except that I was home alone at the time. It only occurred to me after I was in the suitcase that it would have been wise to have someone nearby to call for help, if I needed it."

FIVE

THE CHARACTER'S LIFE

Critics often note Haddix's ability to create well-developed characters. Her skill likely began as a young reader. She liked books with realistic characters. "The people I met in books always seemed very real to me," she says on her Web site.

So, the author strives to make her own characters as human as possible, and her characters do seem real. For example, *Kirkus Reviews* described the protagonist in *Dexter the Tough* as a "sympathetic and believable character." *Booklist's* review of *Among the Imposters* said, "Luke and his

MARGARET PETERSON
HADDIX

author of *Running Out of Time*

just
Ella

Happily Never After…

Just Ella offers a modern take on the Cinderella fairy tale. Critics praised the novel for Haddix's well-developed characters, creative plot twists, wit, and drama.

experiences are believable in the appealing, simple futuristic story." And a *Booklist* review of *Just Ella* says, "In lively prose, with well-developed characters, creative plot twists, wit, and drama, Haddix transforms the Cinderella tale into an insightful coming of age story."

REVEALING CHARACTER

The most realistic characters have what writers call three dimensions. A three-dimensional character is a fictional character portrayed in a lifelike manner. Not every character needs this treatment. Characters who spend most of their time on the sidelines need only quick sketches. They exist to give major players someone to talk to. And their actions move the plot along.

However, heroes and villains certainly need the full treatment. That starts with what the world sees. What do they look like? What are their personalities? What quirky traits or habits do they have?

Jonah Skidmore is the main character in *the Missing* series. At first, readers get little description—he's a tall guy with brown hair. But Jonah is going to be around for several books. Haddix reveals his personality a little at a time. Readers will have to wait to learn who he really is and what is behind his behavior.

MARGARET PETERSON HADDIX'S AWARDS

- International Reading Association's Children's Book Award
- American Library Association Best Book
- Young Adult Library Services Quick Pick for Reluctant Young Adult Readers
- Notable Trade Book in the Field of Social Studies
- New York Public Library Book for the Teen Age
- American Bestseller Pick of the Lists
- Eleanor Cameron Award for Middle Grades
- State readers' choice lists in over twenty-eight states

Another aspect of a character is his or her backstory. A backstory is what happened before the main story started. It includes past experiences that influence his or her current behavior. It may also include whatever secrets they're hiding. In *Found*, the first book in *the Missing* series, Jonah gets a six-word letter that says, "You are one of the missing." His seventh-grade friend Chip Winston thinks that Jonah got the letter because he was adopted. But Chip gets the same letter. He tells his father about

Jonah's letter and his first idea that Jonah got it because he was adopted. He tells his dad that the letter must not be about being adopted "because *I* got the same letter, and *I'm* not adopted." Then he says, "Right, Dad? I'm not adopted, am I, Dad?"

The backstory revelation affects how Chip reacts to the situation as the plot advances.

The final element needed to create a realistic character is the person's moral substance and worldview. In *The Girl with 500 Middle Names*, Janie's mother has been knitting sweaters for a year. She hopes that by selling them she can enable the family to move so that Janie can go to a better school in a more affluent area. Janie's father keeps saying that money isn't everything, but Janie has outgrown her clothes. Her mother takes her shopping, even though none of her sweaters has sold. Haddix reveals Janie's moral substance through Janie's narration: "All I could see was Momma's hands. I remembered how she'd knitted and knitted and knitted, early in the morning and late at night, on the bus and at home, every second she could for a solid year. Just for me. Because she loved me. I thought maybe Daddy was right, after all, and some things did matter more than money. And then I knew what I had to do. 'Momma,' I started. I cleared my throat. 'Momma, I don't need any new clothes.'"

FEELING CLOSE TO A CHARACTER

Just as authors must believe events in a book are real, they must also believe in the people who populate their imaginary worlds.

In *Don't You Dare Read This, Mrs. Dunphrey*, Haddix had nothing in common with Tish, the protagonist. Still, Haddix felt close to her. "I did feel possessed by Tish's spirit," she said in *Something About the Author*. "Actually, in a way, everything I've written has felt like that, like being possessed."

She elaborated further in *Major Authors and Illustrators for Young Children*. "A lot of times when I'm doing the ordinary things that go along with having two kids, a husband, and a house—cooking, playing chauffer, running to Wal-Mart—I'm listening to a voice inside my head insisting, 'Write about me!' ... Now, I'll be the first to admit that it sounds a little weird to have voices talking in my head, but I wouldn't have it any other way."

One such character "spoke" to the author when she was writing *Found*. At first, Haddix thought Katherine would be only a minor character. However, Haddix told Cynthia Leitich Smith in an interview for her blog that Katherine kept pestering her. The imaginary character would "say" things like, "Hey, you really need me in this scene, too … I'm going in whether you want me to or not."

Eventually, Haddix gave in and Katherine got a much bigger role in the story.

WHAT'S IN A NAME?

Naming characters often presents another challenge to Haddix. "When I was a little kid, my favorite doll was named Susie Egg," she told the Teen Book Festival. "My family would tell you that my character-naming skills have not improved since then."

But that doesn't keep her from trying. For *Running Out of Time*, she gave characters names that were common in both the 1840s and 1990s. "Jessie would have gotten very strange looks in the world outside Clifton if her name had been, say, Mehitabel," Haddix told ThinkQuest.

Haddix used the ethnic names Bella and Yetta for Italian and Russian immigrants in *Uprising*. Characters in *the Shadow Children* series have such names as Luke, Trey, George, Nina, Matthias, Melly, Anny Beth, and Jen. The time-traveling characters in *the Missing* series are called Jonah, Katherine, Chip, Alex, and JB. Many of these characters appear in more than one book in the series.

Some other Haddix characters include Sukie in *Say What?*; KT in *Game Changer*; Anya in *Because*

MARGARET PETERSON HADDIX

Author of *Among the Hidden*

Running Out of Time

An ALA Best Book for Young Adults

For *Running Out of Time*, Haddix chose names that were common in both the nineteenth and twentieth centuries. In other books, she gives names she likes to characters she likes.

of Anya; and Bethany, Elizabeth, and Aunt Myrlie in *Double Identity*.

"For the most part, I gave names I liked to characters I liked," Haddix told ThinkQuest. "With other books I've sometimes resorted to using a baby name book to find first names and the phone book to find last names."

ACTION AND DIALOGUE

Readers learn about characters by what the characters say, what they do, and what other characters say about them. Haddix is a master at using all three techniques to help readers get to know her characters.

The author uses lively, age-appropriate dialogue that real kids would use. In *Leaving Fishers*, the main character, Dorry, is talking with her friend Zachary about Fishers, the religious cult she has been involved with:

Zachary snorted "You really were an easy mark for Fishers, weren't you, Miss Gullible?" He shook his head. "Sorry, I thought you were smarter than that. Ever notice the offering plate at Fishers services?"

"Sure, but—"

"Pastor Jim's got a lot of money, thanks to Fishers. He's got practically a mansion up in Carmel—"

Dorry wasn't ready to believe that. "No, he's got an apartment in a bad part of the city. He talks about it all the time."

"That's just for show … You didn't give a lot of money to Fishers, did you?"

Dorry looked away. "My college savings," she said.

To create believable dialogue, Haddix listens to the way real people talk. "Dialogue is one of the most important writing ways of establishing character," the author told ThinkQuest. "So if you want to be able to write good dialogue, you have to listen to what people really sound like."

Character action is another way to show readers a character's quirks and traits. In *Found*, readers see that, like many teens, Jonah can be a bit self-conscious: "Jonah fell into the grass laughing. After a moment, Chip started laughing, too. It was like being a little kid again, rolling around in the grass laughing, not caring at all about who might see you.

"Jonah stopped laughing and sat up. He peered up and down the street—fortunately, nobody was around to see him. He whacked Chip on the arm."

A third type of information about a character can come from other characters. In *The Girl with 500 Middle Names*, Janie describes her classmate with other classmates' help: "Cross-eyed Krissy looked at me—first with one eye, then the other—and then she spit right on my shoes. Everybody told me I was lucky she didn't beat me up."

Haddix likes writing for young audiences, and she favors characters in their teens. "Teenagers are naturally such good characters in books," she told the *Ohio Reading Road Trip*. "They have great capacity for change, and they're often more interesting than adults."

READING AND WRITING

As a child Margaret learned to enjoy reading because she saw her parents read. Her parents were busy people, but they both still read a lot. "The message they gave us was clear," Haddix told the *Eighth Book of Junior Authors and Illustrators*, "No matter how busy you are, books are worth finding time for. They're fun."

Not surprisingly, Haddix is a strong advocate for reading at all ages. She advises parents to follow her parents' lead. "Reading to children from babyhood on up is incredibly important," she said at the 2010 National Book Festival. "Even when they're reading well on their own, it's great to also read some books along with them. Compare notes on what each of you think about the book."

Haddix encourages parents and other adults to read to children from babyhood on—even after the children learn to read. Along with entertaining the reader, reading improves language and teaches interesting information.

Setting aside a specific reading time to set it apart from the rest of their lives also helps inspire new readers, she said. Reading can get lost in a busy life full of other activities.

Before Margaret went to college, her school never required summer reading lists. Because of that—then and now as an adult—she thinks summer is the best time to read for fun. Along with entertainment value, books offered interest-ing information. "I think I learned a lot from reading in general—even from reading badly written books," she said on Evi.com.

Still, she doesn't want reading forced on children. In an interview with the *Akron Beacon Journal* reported on Contemporary Authors Online, she discussed library reading pro-grams where children read a certain number of minutes and win a prize at summer's end. "I like seeing the emphasis on reading," she said. "But I'm almost afraid the more we push it, the more young readers will think of it like broccoli or spinach that doesn't taste good or isn't fun. I'd like to see them pick up a book and read it and not think 'I've read for fifteen minutes.' The more they read and begin to enjoy it, the more likely they are to continue."

RELUCTANT READERS

Haddix told Contemporary Authors Online that as a writer her primary goal is to engage readers. But she was surprised to learn that many of her books appeal to reluctant readers.

Although no single definition of the term "reluctant reader" is widely accepted, in general it applies to children who tend to shy away from books and other reading materials, rather than eagerly grab them and read. Several reasons exist for the less-than-enthusiastic attitude.

The reluctance may be due to limited learning experiences, low self-esteem, or a learning disability. According to the New Albany-Floyd County Consolidated School Corporation, reluctant readers generally fall into three categories:

1. Those who like reading but don't have or make time for it.

2. Those who don't like to read but may become future readers.

3. Those who don't like to read and think they never will.

Reviewers who say Haddix's books appeal to reluctant readers cite both her character development and suspenseful plots. Readers care about her characters, and her stories keep readers turning pages. But the author isn't sure how that happens. She knows, however, that when she starts writing a novel, she feels a sense of urgency to tell the story. That urgency may transfer to the reader and give Haddix's novels a suspenseful flavor. That same urgency seems to appeal to reluctant readers.

When Haddix started writing books for young readers, she thought her readers would be the kind who liked to pick up a book and read it—someone like her childhood self. However, she told *Reading Rockets*, "It kind of amazed me when I started getting letters from kids and hearing from teachers that they saw my books as appealing to reluctant readers. And I thought that makes it a lot harder to think that I am writing for kids who don't want to be reading. But I am really gratified when I've heard from kids who say, 'I didn't like to read, but then I read your book and I loved it.' So that's a very good feeling to have."

MARGARET HADDIX'S FAVORITE AUTHORS TODAY

As an adult, Margaret Haddix still loves to read. And she still chooses books from a variety of genres, including historical fiction and science fiction. Her favorite authors today include one name from her childhood list: E. L. Konigsburg. Others include:

Margaret Atwood
Edward Bloor
Barbara Kingsolver
Mary Doria Russell
Neal Shusterman
Cynthia Voight
… and many others.

Writer and artist E. L. Konigsburg was one of Haddix's favorite authors as a child—and later as an adult. Konigsburg won the Newbery Medal for *From the Mixed-Up Files of Mrs. Basil E. Frankweiler.*

That feeling is important to the author. She told Kristy Eckert of *Capital Style* that she considers her greatest accomplishment "turning kids on to reading."

ADVICE FOR YOUNG WRITERS

"Read a lot. Write a lot. Think a lot." Those are Haddix's top three tips for young writers. "I suggest they read as much as they can, so they know what other writers are writing," Haddix told *Something About the Author*. "I also suggest that they play around with writing in different genres, trying out poetry, fiction, nonfiction, etc."

Reading a variety of genres influenced Haddix to write in a variety of genres. Her early reading of science fiction, for example, spurred her to write science fiction. But she also enjoys writing different types of novels. Haddix credits her journalism background and her own interests as also contributing to her writing in different genres. "I enjoy exploring lots of different subjects," she said in *Major Authors and Illustrators for Children and Young Adults*. "And I hope that kids do, too."

It seems they do. The author's awards and book sales speak for themselves.

Haddix tells young writers to find time to sit and just think—and to record their thoughts in a journal. "Listen carefully and observe the world," she told ThinkQuest. "Pay attention to how people talk, what they say, and how they say it. And pay attention to the world around you. It's hard to describe, say, beautiful flowers, if you've really never noticed them."

GETTING STARTED

At the 2010 National Book Festival, Haddix offered two exercises to get young writers started on their own stories:

- Imagine that you're somebody else. Write a story from that character's perspective. "Choose a character who is bolder, braver, or louder than you," she said. "Or, choose someone quieter or shyer."
- Write about a disagreement you've had— from the other person's viewpoint. See how much the story changes.

Finally, she told *Reading Rockets*, writers must be able and willing to take suggestions for revision. "It's very hard for any writers at any level to accept criticism of their work. I know when I was a kid, I was very sensitive about what I'd written, and because I had poured my heart and soul into it … I thought of it as a masterpiece."

HOW LONG DOES IT TAKE TO WRITE A BOOK?

Haddix usually spends two to six months on her first draft of a new novel. Then she sets it aside for a while to gain some distance from it. When she comes back to the manuscript, she sees it with fresh eyes. That makes it easier to spot places she can improve it.

Revision usually takes as long as writing—or longer. "Sometimes I can spend as long revising a manuscript as I spent writing it in the first place," Haddix told Evi.com. For instance, she spent six months revising *Running Out of Time* before she started sending it out to agents and editors. In fact, revision continued after the manuscript sold to her publisher. Once a book is in production, she works with her editor at Simon & Schuster to make even more changes.

She advised teachers to be aware of that tendency, especially with young writers. And she advised young writers to see their writing as something that can be improved. "If someone says, well, this needs to be fixed," she continued in the interview, "that doesn't mean that you are saying the whole thing is terrible and you're a terrible writer. It's just: let's make it as good as possible. But, that is something that is very hard to learn because writing is such a personal thing."

LOOKING BACK AND AHEAD

In an interview for her blog, Cynthia Leitich Smith asked Haddix what advice she would give to her younger self when she was a beginning writer. Not surprisingly, Haddix jumped at the chance to participate in that sort of time travel.

Her answer: "Stop spending so much time wondering whether you're a journalist or a fiction writer. It's all writing! You're a writer! Just write!"

Haddix added that she would have liked to hear that her books would be published—that everything would work out. However, she said, if she had known that, she's not sure that she would have tried so hard.

Today, Haddix is a full-time, working writer. As Haddix thinks back on her career so far, she told Cynthia Leitich Smith, "I was somewhat surprised that writing fiction wasn't pure, unadulterated joy every single moment. But I've been delighted at how often it does feel like that."

Her career as a writer—the one she dreamed of as a child, but never thought she could have—continues. She always has something in the works, often more than one novel at a time. She may be

Haddix advises young writers to find time to sit and think and record their thoughts in a journal. A journal is also a good place to take down real-life conversations and observations about the world.

finishing a first draft on one, revising another, or getting one ready for publication. Her persistence drives her forward. So does her basic instinct. As she said in *Something About the Author*, "When I'm writing, I feel like I *must* write."

ON MARGARET PETERSON HADDIX

Birth date: April 9, 1964

Birthplace: Washington Court House, Ohio

Grew up: Farm near Washington Court House, Ohio

Father's occupation: Farmer

Mother's occupation: Nurse

Siblings: Two brothers and one sister

Current residence: Columbus, Ohio

First book: *Running Out of Time* (Simon & Schuster)

Marital status: Married

Husband's occupation: Training director, Investigative Reporters and Editors

Children: Meredith and Connor

College attended: Miami University of Ohio

Memberships: Society of Children's Book Writers and Illustrators and Phi Beta Kappa Society

Hobbies: Reading, traveling, swimming, bicycling, hiking, visiting museums

Web site: http://www.haddixbooks.com

ON MARGARET PETERSON HADDIX'S WORK

Series: *The Shadow Children*

The Shadow Children series is a collection of books about Luke Garner. He is the third child of his family, and in his world families cannot have more than two children. Luke lives "among the hidden," which is the title of the first book. But population police search out third children, while Luke hides, runs, and survives.

1. *Among the Hidden* (1998)
2. *Among the Imposters* (2001)
3. *Among the Betrayed* (2002)
4. *Among the Barons* (2003)
5. *Among the Brave* (2004)
6. *Among the Enemy* (2005)
7. *Among the Free* (2006)

FACT SHEET

Series: *The Missing*
A plane full of babies lands in the wrong time zone —as in the wrong century! They are the "missing" children who were adopted in that time period. Later, someone comes from the future hunting them, and the children learn about their past.

1. *Found* (2008)
2. *Sent* (2009)
3. *Sabotaged* (2010)
4. *Torn* (2011)
5. *Caught* (2012)
6. *Risked* (2013)

Other Novels
Running Out of Time (1995)
Don't You Dare Read This, Mrs. Dunphrey (1996)
Leaving Fishers (1997)
Just Ella (1999)
Turnabout (2000)
The Girl with 500 Middle Names (2001)
Takeoffs and Landings (2001)
Because of Anya (2002)
Escape from Memory (2003)
Say What? (2004)
The House on the Gulf (2004)

Double Identity (2005)

Dexter the Tough (2007)

Uprising (2007)

Palace of Mirrors (2008)

Claim to Fame (2009)

Into the Gauntlet: Book 10, The *39 Clues* series (2010)

The Always War (2011)

Game Changer (2012)

Full Ride (2013)

Running Out of Time (1995)

"Absorbing and gripping. The action moves swiftly, with plenty of suspense."—*School Library Journal*

Don't You Dare Read This, Mrs. Dunphrey (1996)

"Breezy style, short diary-entry format, and melodramatic subject matter will ensure popularity for this title, particularly with reluctant readers."— *Voice of Youth Advocates*

Among the Barons (2003)

"There is enough background information in the opening chapter to fill in readers new to the series, and series fans won't be disappointed; there's plenty of suspense, and there are lots of thrilling twists and turns."—*Booklist*, May 15, 2003

The House on the Gulf (2004)

"A subtle mystery builds to a surprising climax with enough twists to keep readers guessing along the way."—*Kirkus Reviews*, August 1, 2004

Among the Brave (2004)

"Haddix writes a compelling story, full of intrigue, danger and adventure. The level of tension barely lets up, ensuring that 'can't-put-it-down' headlong impulse to keep reading."—*Booklist*, May 15, 2004

Double Identity (2005)

"Haddix conveys Bethany's dismay and fear through believable dialogue and thoughts." — *Publisher's Weekly*

Claim to Fame (2009)

"The veteran writer has the ability to make her characters recognizable even with brief sketches, and she holds attention with the mounting suspense." — *Kirkus Reviews*, October 1, 2009

Sabotaged (2010)

"Haddix concentrates more on the action, suspense, and mystery ... the plot is internally consistent, too, enhancing both pace and readers' enjoyment. Best of the series so far." — *Kirkus Reviews*, July 1, 2011

Torn (2011)

"Haddix keeps the story suspenseful and tight. Best of all, the story feels like real history, with believable characters and plausible events." — *Kirkus Reviews*, July 1, 2011

The Always War (2011)

"A fast-paced story line with many end-of-chapter cliffhangers urging the reader to continue. Tessa is likable and believable, complete with both dreams and a few flaws." — Teenreads.com

1964 Margaret Peterson is born on April 9.

1983 She graduates from Miami Trace High School in Washington Court House, Ohio; wins honorable mention in *Seventeen* magazine's fiction writing contest.

1984 She works as an assistant cook at a 4-H camp.

1985 She serves a summer internship at the *Urbana Daily Citizen* in Urbana, Ohio.

1986 She serves a summer internship at the *Charlotte Observer* in Charlotte, North Carolina.

1987 She graduates from Miami University of Ohio; works as a copy editor at the *Fort Wayne Journal-Gazette* in Indiana; marries Doug Haddix on October 3; works as a reporter for the *Indianapolis News* in Indiana.

1991 She decides to write fiction, as well as nonfiction freelance writing; works part-time teaching writing as an adjunct faculty member for Danville Area Community College in Illinois.

1995 Her first book, *Running Out of Time*, is published; she becomes a full-time writer.

2002 She publishes tenth and eleventh books, *Among the Betrayed* and *Because of Anya*.

2004 Simon & Schuster threatens to sue the makers of M. Night Shyamalan's film *The Village* over alleged similarities with the plot of her first novel *Running Out of Time*.

2007 She publishes twentieth and twenty-first books, *Dexter the Tough* and *Uprising*.

2014 She publishes thirtieth book.

GLOSSARY

ADJUNCT FACULTY A faculty member who works only part-time.

BEAT REPORTER A newspaper reporter assigned to a specific subject area.

BOOK SERIES A group of books that have characteristics in common. They may be written by the same author or share the same characters or be organized and marketed as a group.

CHARACTERIZATION The creation and description of a fictional character.

COLLEGE MAJOR A college student's chosen field of study where his or her interest and efforts are concentrated.

COPYRIGHT Literally, the right to copy; the exclusive legal right to publish or perform a work of art.

COSMOLOGIST A scientist who deals with the origin, structure, and space-time relationships of the universe.

FICTIVE DREAM A subconscious activity similar to daydreaming, when a reader becomes so absorbed in the world the author created that the fiction seems to become reality.

4-H A youth development organization that seeks to teach leadership, citizenship, and life skills with hands-on learning experiences.

FREELANCE WRITER A self-employed writer who sells work to newspapers, magazines, or businesses without a long-term commitment to any of them.

GENERAL ASSIGNMENT REPORTER A newspaper or broadcast employee who covers a wide variety of stories.

GENRE A category of literature or other artistic work that has a particular style, form, or content.

INTERNSHIP An on-the-job type of training where a student or recent graduate gains supervised, hands-on experience in his or her field of study.

JOURNALISM The collection, writing, and editing of news to be distributed via news media.

LITERARY AGENT An author's representative who looks for a publisher for a manuscript and negotiates the contract.

"LOST YEARS" A seven-year period in the sixteenth century where no records exist about poet and playwright William Shakespeare's life.

MIDDLE AGES The period of European history between the fifth and fifteenth centuries.

PHI BETA KAPPA SOCIETY An academic honor society for college students in liberal arts and sciences.

PLAGIARISM The act of claiming someone else's words or ideas as one's own without giving credit to the original source.

PRIMARY SOURCES Original materials such as interviews, original documents, or artifacts that are free from another's evaluation—sources that other research is based on.

PROTAGONIST The main character in a literary work; the hero or heroine whom the reader identifies with.

RELUCTANT READER A child who shies away from books, rather than eagerly moving toward them.

SHORT STORY A piece of fiction, usually shorter than ten thousand words, focused on a single theme.

SPACE-TIME A model in physics that contains both space and time dimensions. Most commonly, three dimensions of space and one of time. The first system was theorized in 1907, two years after Einstein's theory of relativity was introduced.

SUMMA CUM LAUDE An educational distinction that applies to academic degrees and that means "with highest honor."

THREE-DIMENSIONAL CHARACTER A fictional character portrayed in a lifelike manner.

WILLING SUSPENSION OF DISBELIEF The setting aside of reality for the duration of a play, a movie, or a book in order to accept and enjoy fictional events and characters.

YOUNG ADULT (YA) FICTION Fiction meant for readers between the ages of twelve and eighteen.

Academy of American Poets
75 Maiden Lane, Suite 901
New York, NY 10038
(212) 274-9427
E-mail: academy@poets.org
Web site: http://www.poets.org
The Academy of American Poets supports poets at
all stages of their careers. It was founded in 1934
to encourage the appreciation of contemporary
poetry. It provides programs, as well as online
educational resources.

American Society of Journalists and Authors (ASJA)
Times Square
1501 Broadway, Suite 403
New York, NY 10036
(212) 997-0947
Web site: http://www.asja.org
The ASJA is a national professional organization for
independent nonfiction writers. It offers benefits
and services aimed at professional development.

The Authors Guild
31 East 32nd Street, 7th Floor
New York, NY 10016
(212) 563-5904
E-mail: staff@authorsguild.org
Web site: http://www.authorsguild.org
The Authors Guild is an organization that advocates
for writers and provides legal assistance to members. Its focus is effective copyright protection,
fair contracts, and free expression.

Canadian Authors Association (CAA)
74 Mississaga St. East
Orillia, ON L3V 1V5
Canada
(705) 653-0323
E-mail: admin@canauthors.org
Web site: http://www.canauthors.org
The CAA is a national organization of Canadian writers
of all kinds. It recognizes writers and their works,
sponsors awards, and represents writers before
government bodies to improve copyright protection.

Investigative Reporters and Editors (IRE)
141 Neff Annex
Missouri School of Journalism
Columbia, MO 65211
(573) 882 2042
E-mail: info@ire.org
Web site: http://www.ire.org
Founded in 1975 in Reston, Virginia, the IRE is a
nonprofit organization dedicated to improving the
quality of investigative journalism by sharing tips,
resources, and training.

National 4-H Headquarters
U.S. Department of Agriculture
National Institute of Food and Agriculture
1400 Independence Avenue SW, Stop 2201
Washington, DC 20250-2201
(800) 333-4636
Web site: http://www.4-H.org
4-H is a youth development organization with more
than six million members. It teaches leadership,

citizenship, and life skills. It began in agricultural areas but now also serves suburban and urban communities.

National League of American Pen Women
National Headquarters–Pen Arts Building
1300 17th Street NW
Washington, DC 20036-1973
(202) 785-1997
E-mail: contact@nlapw.org
Web site: http://www.nlapw.org
The National League of American Pen Women is a nonprofit organization for women who are professional artists, writers, composers, and choreographers. It encourages, recognizes, and promotes production of creative work.

Phi Beta Kappa Society
1606 New Hampshire Avenue NW
Washington, DC 20009
(202) 265-3808
Web site: https://www.pbk.org/home
Phi Beta Kappa is an academic honor society founded in 1776 for college students who excel in the liberal arts and sciences.

Professional Writers Association of Canada (PWAC)
215 Spadina Avenue, Suite 130
Toronto, ON MST 2C7
Canada
(416) 504-1645
E-mail: info@pwac.ca
Web site: http://www.pwac.ca

The PWAC is a national nonprofit organization of free-lance writers in Canada's magazine and newspaper industries.

Romance Writers of America (RWA)
14615 Benfer Road
Houston, TX 77069
(832) 717-5200
E-mail: info@rwa.org
Web site: http://www.rwa.org/
The RWA is a nonprofit trade association founded to advance the creative and professional growth of romance writers. It supports its members through advocacy and networking. It has more than 10,000 members in 145 local and online chapters.

Science Fiction Writers of America (SFWA)
P.O. Box 3238
Enfield, CT 06083-3238
Web site: http://www.sfwa.org
Science Fiction Writers of America is a professional organization for authors, artists, editors, and other industry professionals who produce works of science fiction, fantasy, and related genres. It hosts the Nebula Awards.

Sisters in Crime
P.O. Box 442124
Lawrence, KS 66044
(785) 842-1325
E-mail: admin@sistersincrime.org
Web site: http://www.sistersincrime.org
With 3,600 members in 48 chapters worldwide,

Sisters in Crime promotes the professional development of women crime writers.

Society of Children's Book Writers & Illustrators (SCBWI)
8271 Beverly Blvd.
Los Angeles, CA 90048
(323) 782-1010
E-mail: scbwi@scbwi.org
Web site: http://www.scbwi.org
The SCBWI is an international nonprofit professional organization for writers and illustrators in the fields of literature, magazines, film, television, and multimedia for children and young adults.

Society of Professional Journalists (SPJ)
Eugene S. Pulliam National Journalism Center
3909 N. Meridian Street
Indianapolis, IN 46208
(317) 927-8000
Web site: http://spj.org
The Society of Professional Journalists is an organization of professional reporters that seeks to perpetuate a free press in the United States and protect First Amendment rights.

WEB SITES

Due to the changing nature of Internet links, Rosen Publishing has developed an online list of Web sites related to the subject of this book. This site is updated regularly. Please use this link to access the list:

http://www.rosenlinks.com/AAA/haddix

FOR FURTHER READING

Bell, James Scott. *Revision and Self-Editing*. Cincinnati, OH: Writer's Digest Books, 2008.

Card, Orson Scott. *Elements of Fiction Writing— Characters & Viewpoint*. Cincinnati, OH: Writer's Digest Books, 2010.

Card, Orson Scott. *The Writer's Digest Guide to Science Fiction & Fantasy*. Cincinnati, OH: Writer's Digest Books, 2010.

Clark, Roy Peter. *How to Write Short: Word Craft for Fast Times*. New York, NY: Little, Brown, 2012.

Clark, Roy Peter. *Writing Tools*. New York, NY: Little Brown, 2006.

Del Vecchio, Gene. *Creating Blockbusters!* Gretna, LA: Pelican Publishing Company, 2012.

Dethier, Brock. *Twenty-One Genres and How to Write Them*. Logan, UT: Utah State University Press, 2013.

Ephron, Hallie. *The Everything Guide to Writing Your First Novel*. Avon, MA: Adams Media, 2011.

Forbes, Kathryn. *Mama's Bank Account*. New York, NY: Harcourt, 1971.

Ford, Glenn. *Writers Block Demolition*. Mississauga and Oakville, ON, Canada: TrainingNOW, 2012.

Gerke, Jeff. *Write Your Novel in a Month: How to Complete a First Draft in 30 Days and What to Do Next*. Cincinnati OH: Writers Digest Books, 2013.

Halverson, Deborah. *Writing Young Adult Fiction for Dummies*. Hoboken, NJ: Wiley Publishing, 2011.

Hambleton, Vicki, and Cathleen Greenwood. *So, You Want to Be a Writer? How to Write, Get Published, and Maybe Even Make It Big!* New York, NY: Aladdin/Beyond Words, 2012.

Ingermanson, Randy, and Peter Economy. *Writing Fiction for Dummies*. Hoboken, NJ: Wiley Publishing, 2010.

King, Stephen. *On Writing*. New York, NY: Pocket Books, 2010.

Kooser, Ted. *The Poetry Home Repair Manual*. Lincoln, NE: University of Nebraska Press, 2005.

Lamott, Anne. *Bird by Bird*. New York, NY: Anchor Books, 1995.

Lovelace, Maud Hart. *Heaven to Betsy/Betsy in Spite of Herself*. New York, NY: Harper Collins, 2009.

Price, Stephen D. *The Little Black Book of Writers' Wisdom*. New York, NY: Skyhorse Publishing, 2013.

Quillen, Linda. *How I Wrote My First Novel*. Kingsport, TN: Paladin Timeless Books, 2011.

Rothfuss, Peter. *The Name of the Wind*. New York, NY: DAW Trade, 2009.

Smith, Jack. *Write and Revise for Publication*. Cincinnati, OH: Writer's Digest Books, 2013.

Strunk, William, and E. B. White. *The Elements of Style*. 50th anniversary ed. White Plains, NY: Longman, 2008.

Tan, Amy. *The Bonesetter's Daughter*. New York, NY: Ballantine Books, 2008.

Thom, James Alexander. *The Art and Craft of Writing Historical Fiction*. Cincinnati, OH: Writer's Digest Books, 2010.

White, Fred. *Where Do You Get Your Ideas? A Writer's Guide to Transforming Notions Into Narratives*. Cincinnati, OH: Writer's Digest Books, 2012.

Writer's Digest Books Editors. *The Complete Handbook of Novel Writing: Everything You Need to Know About Creating & Selling Your Work.* Cincinnati, OH: Writer's Digest Books, 2010.

Writer's Digest Books Editors. *Writer's Digest University: Everything You Need to Write and Sell Your Work.* Cincinnati, OH: Writer's Digest Books, 2010.

Zinsser, William. *On Writing Well.* New York, NY: HarperCollins, 2006.

Anderson, Stuart. "The Books That Rock the Cradle: Libertarian Themes in Children's Fiction." *Reason*, Vol. 37, No. 8, January 2006, p. 52.

Contemporary Authors Online. "Margaret Peterson Haddix." 2008. Retrieved December 6, 2012 (http://go.galegroup.com.ezproxy.jocolibrary.org/ps/i.do?id=gale%7ch10001223765&v=2.1&u=jcl_dialin&it=r&p=gps&sw=w).

Drew, Bernard A. *100 More Popular Young Adult Authors*. Greenwood Village, CO: Libraries Unlimited, 2002.

Eckert, Kristy. "The (World-Famous, Award-Winning) Author Next Door." *Capital Style*. Retrieved January 23, 2013 (http://www.capital-style.com/content/stories/2009/10/16/1016_trendsetter_haddix.html).

Evi.com. "Facts About Margaret Haddix." Retrieved December 8, 2012 (http://www.evi.com/q/facts_about__margaret_haddix).

FantasticFiction.com. "Margaret Peterson Haddix." Retrieved February 15, 2013 (http://www.fantasticfiction.co.uk/h/margaret-peterson-haddix).

Haddix, Margaret Peterson. "Author Voices." Margaret Peterson Haddix Blog at Simon & Schuster. November 15, 2008. Retrieved December 8, 2012 (http://authors.simonandschuster.com/Margaret-Peterson-Haddix/20539155/voice).

Haddix, Margaret Peterson. "Biography." Official Web Site of Author Margaret Peterson Haddix. July 9,

2012. Retrieved January 23, 2013 (http://www.haddixbooks.com/bio.html).

Haddix, Margaret Peterson. "Top Five Tips for Writing." ThinkQuest. Retrieved December 8, 2012 (http://library.thinkquest.org/J0110073/Author.html).

Library of Congress. "Margaret Peterson Haddix." 2010 National Book Festival. Retrieved December 6, 2012 (http://www.loc.gov/bookfest/kids-teachers/authors/margaret_peterson_haddix).

New Albany Floyd County Consolidated School Corporation. "Parents Tip Sheets Motivate the Reluctant Reader." February 8, 2013. Retrieved February 23, 2013 (http://www.nafcs.k12.in.us/default.asp?q_areaprimaryid=7&q_areasecondaryid=98&q_areatertiaryid=110).

Ohio Reading Road Trip. "Margaret Peterson Haddix." Retrieved December 8, 2012 (http://orrt.org/haddix).

Pavao, Kate. "Margaret Peterson Haddix (Spring Attractions)." Publishers Weekly, April 1, 2002. Information Science and Library Issues Collection. Retrieved December 6, 2012 (http://go.galegroup.com.ezproxy.jocolibrary.org/ps/i.do?id=gale%7CA84650986&v=2.1&u=jcl_dialin&it=r&p=GPS&sw=w).

Reading Rockets. "Margaret Peterson Haddix." 2008. Retrieved December 8, 2012 (http://www.readingrockets.org/books/interviews/haddix).

Reyes, Laurisa White. "Giveaway & Interview w/ Margaret Peterson Haddix." September 30, 2012. Retrieved December 9, 2012 (http://1000wrongs.

blogspot.com/2012/09/giveaway-interview-w-margaret-peterson.html).

Rockman, Connie C. *Eighth Book of Junior Authors and Illustrators*. New York, NY: The H. W. Wilson Company, 2000.

SimonandSchuster.com. "Margaret Peterson Haddix Revealed." Retrieved January 23, 2013 (http://authors.simonandschuster.com/Margaret-Peterson-Haddix/20539155/author_revealed).

Smith, Cynthia Leitich.. "Author Interview: Margaret Peterson Haddix." *Cynsations*, April 22, 2008. Retrieved December 6, 2012 (http://cynthialeitichsmith.blogspot.com/2008/04/author-interview-margaret-peterson.html).

Teen Book Festival. "Meet Margaret Peterson Haddix." Retrieved February 18, 2013 (http://www.teenbookfestival.org/?pg=AuthorBio&ID=118http://www.teenbookfestival.org/?pg=AuthorBio&ID=118http://www.teenbookfestival.org/?pg=AuthorBio&ID=118).

USA Today. "'Village' Plot Looks Too Familiar to Author, Publisher." August 10, 2004. Retrieved February 15, 2013 (http://usatoday30.usatoday.com/money/media/2004-08-10-village-suit_x.htm).

YouTube.com. "Margaret Peterson Haddix: 2010 National Book Festival." October 8, 2010. Retrieved December 6, 2012 (http://www.youtube.com/watch?v=42rvMR2MVJU).

INDEX

ABOUT THE AUTHOR

Mary-Lane Kamberg is a professional writer who started writing in second grade. Like Margaret Peterson Haddix, Kamberg also read everything as a child—including the backs of cereal boxes. She is the author of *The I Love to Write Book: Ideas and Tips for Young Writers* (Crickhollow Books, 2008). She founded and directed the Kansas City Writers Group's I Love to Write Camp for young writers.

PHOTO CREDITS

Cover, pp. 3, 7 The Backstage Studio; pp. 11, 25, 32, 55, 61, 67 Simon & Schuster; pp. 12–13 altrendo travel /Getty Images; pp. 16, 50–51 Carnegie Public Library, Washington Court House, Ohio; p. 19 Time & Life Pictures /Getty Images; pp. 28–29 Buyenlarge/Archive Photos /Getty Images; p. 35 Tara Moore/Stone/Getty Images; pp. 38–39 Goh Chai Hin/AFP/Getty Images; pp. 44–45 Dennis K. Johnson/Lonely Planet Images/Getty Images; p. 47 Duncan Walker/E+/Getty Images; pp. 55-53 Popperfoto/Getty Images; pp. 58–59 Frank Scherschel /Time & Life Pictures/Getty Images; pp. 72–73 Stock Connection/Superstock; p. 77 © AP Images; pp. 82–83 Jupiter Images/Comstock/Thinkstock; cover and interior pages background (marbleized texture) javarman /Shutterstock.com; cover and interior pages (book) www. iStockphoto.com/Andrzej Tokarski; interior pages background (landscape) © iStockphoto.com/Michael Westhoff

Designer: Nicole Russo; Editor: Bethany Bryan
Photo Researcher: Marty Levick